"Genius is the ability to put into effect what is in your mind. There is no other definition of it. - F"
Scott Fitzgerald

The Master Plan

The Master Plan

Author:
JOHNNY GILLESPIE

FIND ME
Johnnygillespiemusic.com

© 2021
All rights reserved.

No part of this book may be reproduce, stored in a retrieval system, or transmitted by any means without the written permission from the author/artist, except by a reviewer who may quote brief passages in a review.

The Master Plan

DEDICATIONS

I want to dedicate this book to those struggling in life, to those who do not know if there is an easy way out. Of course, I wish to further dedicate this book to those who suffer from mental health and see no light. Have faith and know that there is a way, and it's mapped out right before your eyes. Just take the next indicated step and believe in yourself and your journey, and know that it's all part of the master plan

The Master Plan

The Master Plan

THANK YOU'S

I would like to take a moment to thank my wife for being there by my side in my darkest hours and for loving me through it all. My Creator, My friends, my family, my employer, Jeremy Hanna with Sullen, Ronnie King, my mentor John Ford that has taught me most of these principles. Gregg Weatherman, Sasha George for helping walk me through this book process, and to all the people that were not mentioned that changed and helped shape my life, this book would not be possible without you all.

Thank you!

The Master Plan

"Knowledge will give you power,
but character respect" - Bruce lee

How Do You Use This Book?

1. Set a 28-day goal that you want this book to help you achieve.
2. Break it down into daily goals and weekly goals to reach the 28-day goal
3. Read this book as many times it takes
4. Try every one of these concepts until they have become habits.

The Master Plan

The Master Plan

CHAPTER 1
THE TURNING POINT

"The obstacle is the way."

The Master Plan

The Master Plan

Life can challenge you with significant ups-and-downs, but there comes a time when one has reached the turning point. The turning points of being sick and tired; of being sick and tired. It is where that damn rubber meets the road. It is the feeling of things needing to change or else!

You see, for some to change, that is what it takes. You could be one on the other side of things that keeps going and going and commits spiritual suicide repeatedly.

What is your turning point? When is simply enough- enough?

For me, it had nothing to show for all my work. I was tired of being hospitalized from being bi-polar, tired of having to restart every time I had taken that life fall, and tired of the mundane ritual life required. I was in debt; in other words, I was financially broke. Nevertheless, I knew I would never allow things to a breaking point of giving up.

The Master Plan

Deep down, I knew I had to change and change something within. It is like that saying goes, '*A ship without a course is guaranteed to be lost at sea,*' and I was tired of being lost at sea.

I read all the self-help books I could get my hands on, but they did not work. Why? Because I was not taking action, I was not mapping out the destination.

I am that dreamer with a big ass heart that loves to please everyone, would over-commit, and by the end of the day, I was exhausted. I had barely any time for myself and would burn myself out.

I realized it was time for a change, and I had to manage my time better. For starters, I knew I had to make better decisions and prioritize my life more efficiently.

The Master Plan

Money spending habits needed to change, Lifestyle habits needed to change, and goal setting were necessary. Not only that, but I needed to set goals that resonated with me to my core.

This was a considerable epiphany/ awakening for me. To realize something that you have been asking for your whole life was right in front of me the entire time. It was the perfect road map inside that all the great stoics of our time would talk about -- such as *'you become what you think about.'*

In other words, *'what you believe you receive.'* - We will dive into this in a later chapter.

I understood that all pain I experienced happened because the universe had a bigger plan for me than a mundane life. The obstacle is the way.

Where I was, was a deep reflection of lack of planning. As the saying goes, *'failing to plan is planning to fail.'*

I hated when people told me, *'if you work hard, you'll eventually get there.'* Screw that! Work smart by mapping it out, do what you love, and the rest will come to my mantra.

I believe life comes with a pure sense of belief, and I had to get rid of the anxiety, worry, fears, and beliefs that no longer served me that I had stored deep within my subconscious mind.

I had to brainwash my mind and put in the morals, values, and beliefs. I knew to use these new strands of thoughts to serve me for my greatest and highest good. As they say, 'out *with the old and in with the new.'*

I wanted to be covered with the best of best beliefs and have the arsenal ready to dismantle those negative thoughts that distort your mind.

My thought for when negative thinking comes is, '*why to worry about it? It probably won't happen anyway.*' Then boom! I stopped that wrong thought in its tracks, and I level up in keeping my mind clear, fresh and sharp.

I have learned, from past advisements, to run myself like a business and take inventory. A captain that fails to take inventory -- knows his ship could sink. It is critical to know yourself inward and outward. One needs to see every corner of his vessel, treat it with kindness, and realize that what you are reflecting on the inside is now projected on the outward screen of space.

The Master Plan

The Master Plan

Key points to remember:

[x] What's your turning point?

[x] You become what you think about.

[x] Why worry? It probably won't happen.

[x] Take a personal inventory.

[x] Know your vessel.

The Master Plan

The Master Plan

CHAPTER 2
THE ROAD MAP

"Design your life."

The Master Plan

The Master Plan

Of course, the point has led you to be '*the designer of your destiny,*' aka '*the road map.*'

In life, you have to make educated risk backed with unwavering faith. Meaning that you know you, and you know the risk that is reasonable for you to take, but when you do so, have faith that is unshakable when you are doing it!

Do not listen to others. What might work/be valid for one might not work/be right for another? You must take risks and put your faith in them. Listen to your internal navigation system and push the limits of time and space.

Nothing is set in stone. You create your heaven or hell on earth. It all starts with a plan. The plan of not planning is, aka, the drifter in life or one's nightmare. On the other hand, the driver that plans and works with life to let life bring him to his destination, aka heaven on earth!

The Master Plan

- How do you want your life to look?
- What color car do you want to drive?
- Where do you wish to live?

Start by mapping it out! The more descriptive you are the better! Become one with your imagination and internal navigation system and utilize the damn universe, which has given tools and gifts!

Be the grand overall designer of your life because you have a choice to choose what you would like to do or not do. Figure out where you would like your life design to be. Figure out who you want to be and what you stand for.

Do not be like everyone else in the rat race of life. It is a damn trap. That is why they call it a rat race! The primary catch is that you never get the opportunity to fully live and embrace life while you are making someone else happy with his or her dreams at the cost of yours.

The Master Plan

They say the graveyard is the wealthiest place on earth because all those dreams died by those too afraid to seize the day.

Is it your day yet?

Let us face it, we are all going to die one day, so you might as well live fully and embrace the most delicate things in it. It takes courage to live fully! When you are in that alignment with the universe, time stops and works for you instead of you working against time.

Put time into the things you are good at and not what is placed with expectations, from others or mom and dad says you have to do. That is no living, and no one, whom I know likes to inform what to do. It is against every fiber and cell in my body. Stop being compliant with others and be compliant with what your needs and wants are. Those essential gems show you what life is genuinely all about.

The Master Plan

Put that heart of a champion and mind to fair use! I'm talking about laser/ hyper-focus on what it is you desire and map it out!! Dust off that old pen sitting in your drawer, get some paper, and start jotting those ideas down.

A good old fashion pen and paper get those creative forces going, and once they get started, it is on!

Remember, nothing in life is perfect. It is imperfect. So do not be so hard on yourself in the beginning. It is like that saying goes, *'it's not a race to the finish line because everyone sets their own pace.'*

Get a definitive purpose to aim towards those goals. Something that rings that bell in that spirit of gold of yours and contributes to society with the gifts stored within.

The Master Plan

- Do you find meaning in the job or life you currently do and live?

- Are you happy during your working hours or the life you live?

- How do these questions reflect the current work you do or the lifestyle you live?

- In all honesty, to yourself, is it time for a change?

- Maybe these questions provoked your turning point or grand awakening.

- Do you have a hunch to do something but are too afraid of what others around you might say?

These questions might cause some great revelations for you.

Never feel inferior to nature is calling. You have a role in doing, and only you can do it. Be like the director and display what you want to see on the screen of space by directing your film.

Imagine you have a blank canvas now or a second chance, if you will, and on that canvas, you get to draw on it the road map to your vision of success.

Life has its ebbs and flows, such as living the norm of paycheck-to-paycheck or getting past that point by finding the sweet spot of life and living a comfortable and abundant life.

I am talking about dialing in your internal navigation system and trusting in your instincts that most of us have forgotten to use when lost in the rat race of life.

Through time we have been taught to trust others when in actuality, we should be listening to ourselves. *'No one knows you better than you.'*

Let me repeat that *'No one knows you better than you.'*

Why give up your power of choice to someone else? Better yet, why give up your happiness to please someone only temporarily?

To find one's sweet spot or to hone in on one's self-navigation system. One must choose to take charge of his or her ship and learn how to navigate by learning about how feelings impact your mighty vessel and the whole crew on board.

When one is under the deep stresses of life, the ship is under attack. Man must call forth his crew to help tend to the vessel by disarming the negative thoughts and feelings that are harming the ship.

I like to think there are two ways to live either you are surviving in life or your living life as intended!

The Master Plan

Living paycheck to paycheck is living in survival. The sad truth is that is the new norm, and it causes a lot of stress and fears that are unnecessary and damaging to our minds, bodies, and spirits. Trust a belief; *I can relate*.

However, there is a bigger picture in play here, though. Better yet, what if you could live life as intended and make your feelings work for you rather than against you?

Life has its many mysteries that have endless twists and turns. I have experienced the high tides of success with my career Johnny G, and graduating at the top of my class *suma cumladu*. I have experienced the low tides of life by living barely to paycheck to paycheck working for a boss that I disliked and used me and falling due to a disorder that was mentally hard to get back up.

The Master Plan

Why settle for less when in actuality, you could be living for far more!? Know your worth! You are paid based on your self-worth. Meaning what you believe on a subconscious level is what you are currently mentally being paid.

Feel the feeling of wealth and feel the endless possibilities of it. You might have that million-dollar idea you have been praying for, but the question is do you believe in yourself enough to have that leap of faith necessary.

Maybe you keep hitting roadblock after roadblock because you are going about it the wrong way. Perhaps you're too stubborn to re-learn habits that haven't served you well. Maybe the reason you are hitting those roadblocks is that your internal navigation system tells you to go another way or try something different for once.

The definition of insanity:
repeating the same thing over and over again.

Operate your ship and take ownership of your mistakes in life. Do not be afraid and realize the many gifts that the universe is throwing your way for all the things you have asked from it. Maybe the lessons you are experiencing right now are the major lessons you must learn to receive the gift you have asked for.

For example, you are spending money and time that you do not have before you have it.

Now I have been guilty of doing the same thing, and that action alone has cost me countless days of stress and anxiety because it made me barely make rent let alone keeping the sane.

The Master Plan

I like to call it: *Spending before you have it.*

The lesson is to be a good captain of your vessel and take constant inventory of your time, treasure, and talent.

You could spend your time gaining more treasure. Like work, the 9 to 5 or you could put time into your talent/vessel and gain more time and treasure. The choice is yours. What is your point, of course?

The Master Plan

Key points to remember:

- [x] Do what makes you happy.
- [x] How you feel impacts your life.
- [x] Know the value of time, currency & talent.
- [x] Don't settle for less. Know your value
- [x] Be a good captain
- [x] Get detailed about your life.
- [x] Take action.
- [x] Make use of what you have.
- [x] Learn to question for a better life.
- [x] Design your life the way you want it.

The Master Plan

The Master Plan

CHAPTER 3
THROUGH THE STORM

"Wipe away fears and negativity."

The Master Plan

Have you ever had days that were so gloomy and dark that it was impossible to see the light at the end of the tunnel?

I know there are times where it can be challenging to be grateful because everything around you might appear to be falling apart. Fear can be crippling, and thoughts of negativity can run rampant.

I'm here to tell you that you no longer have to batten down the hatches and prepare for trouble because I'm going to tie up loose ends in this chapter. We're going to rock the boat on your beliefs that are hindering your success. We need to unblock the reservoir that connects you to everything that you desire.

There doesn't have to be *two* alternatives between the devil and the deep blue sea.

What if you could learn the ropes and how to sail to the port, aka your chosen destination?

When I finally learned about how my ship worked, everything fell into place. When I took leaps of faith to build self-confidence, that's when miracles followed miracles. It was as if that path laid out for me. Everything connected.

Remember I was telling you about where I was broke, and things weren't going right. That was the moment/beginning of when things began to click together.

You see, it was when I decided to turn my life over to something bigger than me. I realized I needed to partner up with the universe that had everything in it that I desired. The curtains of uncertainty fell to the floor, and finally, I was standing in pure astonishment at the fact that the storm had yet vanished.

The Master Plan

My mind was so clear, and I had a road map laid out before my eyes. I was talking to a buddy that was going through a similar situation. I spoke to others going through the same problem and realized that a lot of people are going through the motions of living paycheck to paycheck.

In my heart, I wanted to help others around me, and it empowered me to write this book. My goal was to bring people together and rise to life and seize the day. But the component that was missing was a book that I could compile all of the information stored within me. You see, the key to success is to keep giving what you know away in hopes that others will succeed in life as well.

We must share our wisdom, knowledge, and experience with others so that they can come to their chosen destination-ports in life as well. Everything must come full circle. That's the way that the world turns. It always goes 'round.

The Master Plan

When I shared what I knew with people who valued my experience, it was rewarding spiritually, but it changed my mindset into something remarkable. I had feelings of happiness. I understood that I was on the right path in life. These quote-on-quote coincidences were not coincidences; they were signs that I was in the right direction.

It's like that old story goes where a man asked another man how to be successful. So the man told the man to follow him into the water.

The man got in the water and then asked: *Now what?*

So the man dunked his head in the water and held him there until he almost passed out...

He then asked: *What do you want now?*

The Master Plan

The man said: *I want to breathe!*

The man said: *Good when you want to live as much as you want to breathe, you will be successful.*

Success breeds success. Successful people want you to be successful, but not all want success as bad as they want to breathe. That's why it's crucial to get rid of the thoughts of fear because, in reality, that is the only thing holding you back in life.

Don't be afraid to fail. Look at failure as a mistake. Get back up and try to take two and three until you get it.

Persistence and momentum will eventually bring you to the place you want to be.

I remember charging someone $200 for something I knew how to do that they didn't know how to do. The customer watched and said, *but that was only* *a $5 part*. I said, *that's right. I charged you $5 for the task and $195 for my time and experience*. But the good thing is, now you know how to do it.

- Did I bring value today?
- Did I not invest in myself for the knowledge?

Get comfortable with being uncomfortable because your comfort always will equal your wealth zone at the end of the day. It would help if you got comfortable and convincing on the price you ask for your time. People will buy it if you have confidence in what you do.

"If you think you can do a thing or think you can't do a thing, you're right." - Henry Ford

Key points to remember:

- [x] Follow your destiny
- [x] Don't be afraid to fail
- [x] Every day is a new opportunity
- [x] Get uncomfortable
- [x] Get paid for confidence

The Master Plan

The Master Plan

CHAPTER 4
THE LAW OF MIND

"What you think, you become."

The Master Plan

Imagine the mind as being fertile soil. That will always return what the farmer plants.

There is a significant rule in life that *'whatever a man plants within his mind will eventually come to fruition.'* and *'what you sow, so shall you reap.'*

If you plant seeds of negativity within yourself, negatively will come back tenfold. On the reverse side of things, you can always grow positively in your mind, and those seeds will eventually see the light and bring abundance and all the wonders you sought in your life.

You plant ideas in your mind by the thoughts, feelings, and actions that you take every day. What you plant goes deep into the soil of your subconscious mind expressing itself into the land you walk on.

Life always comes back to the fundamental belief, which is captured within your subconscious mind.

"Know thyself" know what your weaknesses are and overcome adversity. The better you get to know yourself, the less alone you will be. The opinions of others will no longer affect you for the worst because you know who you are at the end of the day.

If you have the idea of '*I can't*,' reverse the concept into '*I will*.' You are at this point, what you feed your mind. Beware of what you watch on TV, read in the news, or social media because it all comes full circle. '*What goes around always comes around.*'

You have the golden ticket to life and all its wonders within yourself. '*Ask, and you shall receive, seek and you shall find, knock, and the doors of life will be open to you.*'

The Master Plan

What I mean by this is having unwavering faith in what you ask for. Live as if you know it is going to happen. What you are seeking is seeking you, and all you have to do is walk through the door of faith within yourself.

"The mature person strives for strength- the strength of purpose, strength of mind, and strength of character. Only these can give us peace and serenity, joy and accomplishment." -earl nightingale

We are all creators and co-exist with one another, so why not plant seeds of greatness in all aspects of your life. You can start to refresh your mind by giving others what you can.

As I have shared earlier, we can offer three things: time, treasure, or talent. We can always give something.

Giving gives one a sense of happiness, and one is always gifted tenfold the thing he or she passes from the heart. People want to contribute to society. It brings an inner sense of purpose.

When giving, make sure there are no strings attached. Give because you want to provide and watch all the rewards of life come in.

On the other side of things, remember to be a good receiver. When one wants to give, no matter their social status, make sure you receive an open heart. Never look down on one. They are where they are because of the seeds they have sown.

You must be a good receiver and giver to complete the circuit of life. All of life is an exchange of energy. Money is but a symbol for its trade.

Remember what you sow, so shall you reap. To plant seeds of kindness and love into all that you do. Become passionate in the ability to give and receive.

Everything is temporary; what could be yours today could be another's tomorrow.

Never stop the exchange of energy. Energy must always complete its circuit and arrive at its destination.

The Master Plan

Key points to remember:

- [x] Know the laws of mind.

- [x] Give to receive.

- [x] You are born to create.

- [x] Exchange something to gain something.

- [x] Everything is temporary.

The Master Plan

The Master Plan

CHAPTER 5
IGNITE YOUR DESIRE

"How to fuel your ship."

The Master Plan

The Master Plan

Have you heard the saying, don't play with fire, you will get burned? I want to think of that fire representing a person that knows where they are going in life. They will burn you because they are so confident and are unshakable in what it is that they do. Their current is so strong that it is almost impossible to stop that fire from burning to the finish line.

That is how your desire should be impossible to put out or stop. Fire is a magical force that life has gifted each of us. The day it burns out is the day you transition to the next life. I believe we are all here to serve a purpose. That purpose is what I like to call your desire.

So how does one ignite their desire and keep it going?

What if you are so tired and burned out?

It all boils down to this point. Napoleon Hill, in *'think and grow rich,'* states you must find that -- **why**. Your why is the reason you are here.

I will give you an example of a definite purpose:

"I Bruce Lee will be the first highest paid Oriental superstar in the United States. In return, I will give the most exciting performance and render the best of quality in an actor's capacity. Starting 1970, I will achieve world fame, and from then onward till the end of 1980, I will have in my possession $10,000,000. I will live the way I please and achieve inner harmony and happiness."

Bruce Lee | 1969

The Master Plan

Burning desire:

1. (A strong need or must)
2. Bruce Lee had a burning desire to famous

Definite purpose:

1. Ones calling
2. His defined purpose was to be the first highest paid oriental in the USA.

Appropriate action to achieve that purpose.

1. He stated: *"I will give the most exciting performance and render the best of quality in the capacity of an actor. "*

Through thick and thin, Bruce Lee saw that vision through. One must keep their mind fixed on the best because when you do, something magical happens.

- What do you bring to the table?

The Master Plan

Key points to remember:

- [x] Get a burning desire for something

- [x] Find your calling

- [x] Take action on your calling

- [x] What will you give for success?

- [x] What do you bring to the table?

The Master Plan

CHAPTER 6
MASTER YOUR FATE

"Take charge of your destiny."

The Master Plan

The Master Plan

I've come to find that there is a thinking stuff from which all things are made and from thinking in this substance we develop the things we think about. - the science of getting rich

- There is always a higher power at work (and it's on your side).
- Where do you want to go?
- It's like the saying goes the faith of a mustard seed can move mountains
- There's always a cost.

Pay yourself first:

- Take care of yourself so you can take care of others.
- They say: "The grateful mind is constantly fixed on the best."

A man who dares to waste one hour has not discovered the value of life. -Charles Darwin

There is so much power in the spoken word. Here are some words I found to have and add significant value to my life.

Change your words to change your destiny.

Acceptance:
agreement with or belief in an idea, opinion, or explanation.

Courage:
the ability to do something that frightens one.

Perseverance:
persistence in doing something despite difficulty or delay in achieving success.

Cooperation:
the process of working together to the same end. Think win-win and make a good first impression.

Compassion:
Someone showing kindness, care, and a willingness to help others.

Honesty:
The courage to tell the truth

Kindness
the quality of being friendly, generous, and considerate. A kind act.

Integrity:
the quality of being honest and having strong moral principles; moral uprightness.

Power:
Organized energy or effort.

Desire:
a strong feeling of wanting to have something or wishing for something to happen.

Imagination:
the ability of the mind to be creative or resourceful.

Responsibility: the state or fact of being accountable or to blame for something.

Innovate: Embrace failure and keep on trying.

Focus: Be effective, not efficient, and declutter.

Positivity: Live in the present and banish negativity

The Master Plan

List of affirmations:

I can:
being able to. Having confidence in one's self.
(A way of saying yes!)

I can't:
Lack of confidence. Uncertainty

I will:
expressing the future tense.
(Maybe not right now, but I will!)

I won't:
Another way of saying "No"

It is my intention:
Is an idea that you plan (or intend) to carry out. If you mean something, it's an intention

neglect:
Letting go of—the opposite of intention.

"Day by day in every way, I am becoming better and better."

"I am always at the right place at the right time."

"Health, wealth, and success come to me in abundance."

"I always know what I need to know."

The Master Plan

"Today is the day of completion, I give thanks for this perfect day."

"Miracle shall follow miracle, and wonders shall never cease."

"I have perfect work in a perfect way, I give perfect service for perfect pay."

What characteristics do you possess?

Take the helm

Take 100% responsibility for your life.

They say you are the accumulation of the five people you spend the most time with.

We must make up leeway for all the time wasted

Know your ship and all its components. What will you take on board with your fellow crewmates? It's a fact that you are what you eat, say, and do.

Learn to see with the soul. Unless the soul goes out to meet what we know, we do not see it in our own personal reality. We must learn to see within

The Master Plan

Key points to remember:

- [x] Know the power in your word
- [x] Every sentence is an affirmation
- [x] Your word is your bond
- [x] Change your destiny by your word
- [x] Speak with confidence with the willingness to take action.
- [x] Take 100% responsibility for your actions.
- [x] The five people rule.
- [x] You are what you think say and do
- [x] Learn to see it before it happens
- [x] See within to see in reality.

The Master Plan

CHAPTER 7
THE COMPASS

"Your master plan."

The Master Plan

The Master Plan

From poverty to power.

Rise up, Stop feeling sorry for yourself

It's not the years in your life that count. It's the life in your years that counts. - Abraham Lincoln

Key points to remember:

Live life with '*No*' regrets

You are allowed to be anything you want.

Your thoughts are everything.

Love yourself

Questions to ponder in closing:

Do you give up too quickly?

Have you done what you set out to do?

The Master Plan

It is time to take action, my friends! Use this log to help you achieve whatever it is you desire. Get as detailed as you can—best of luck. We challenge you to 4 weeks 28 days to achieve your first goal.

The Master Plan

The Master Plan

Checklist:

[x] What's your turning point?
[x] You become what you think about.
[x] Why worry? It probably won't happen.
[x] Take a personal inventory.
[x] Know your vessel.
[x] Do what makes you happy.
[x] How you feel impacts your life.
[x] Know the value of time, currency & talent.
[x] Don't settle for less. Know your value
[x] Be a good captain
[x] Get detailed about your life.
[x] Take action.
[x] Make use of what you have.
[x] Learn to question for a better life.
[x] Design your life the way you want it.
[x] Follow your destiny
[x] Don't be afraid to fail
[x] Every day, a new opportunity
[x] Get uncomfortable
[x] Get paid for confidence
[x] Know the laws of mind.
[x] Give to receive.
[x] You are born to create.
[x] Exchange something to gain something.
[x] Everything is temporary.

The Master Plan

- [x] Get a burning desire for something
- [x] Find your calling
- [x] Take action on your calling
- [x] What will you give for success?
- [x] What do you bring to the table?
- [x] Know the power in your word
- [x] Every sentence is an affirmation
- [x] Your word is your bond
- [x] Change your destiny by your word
- [x] Speak with confidence with the willingness to take action.
- [x] Take 100% responsibility for your actions.
- [x] The 5 people rule.
- [x] You are what you think say and do
- [x] Learn to see it before it happens
- [x] See within to see in reality.

Final key point:
- [x] The power of habit!

The Master Plan

The Master Plan

What is my 28-day master plan:

What is the aim:

Why do you want to conquer this goal:

When will you accomplish this goal:

The Master Plan

What tools will you require for this goal?:

Who can help you achieve this goal:

28-day goal for yourself:

First 7 day goal:

The Master Plan

Daily log/ captains Ledger | 7 pages for each week

I am grateful for:

1.

_____

2.

_____

3.

_____

The Master Plan

Action plan of the day:

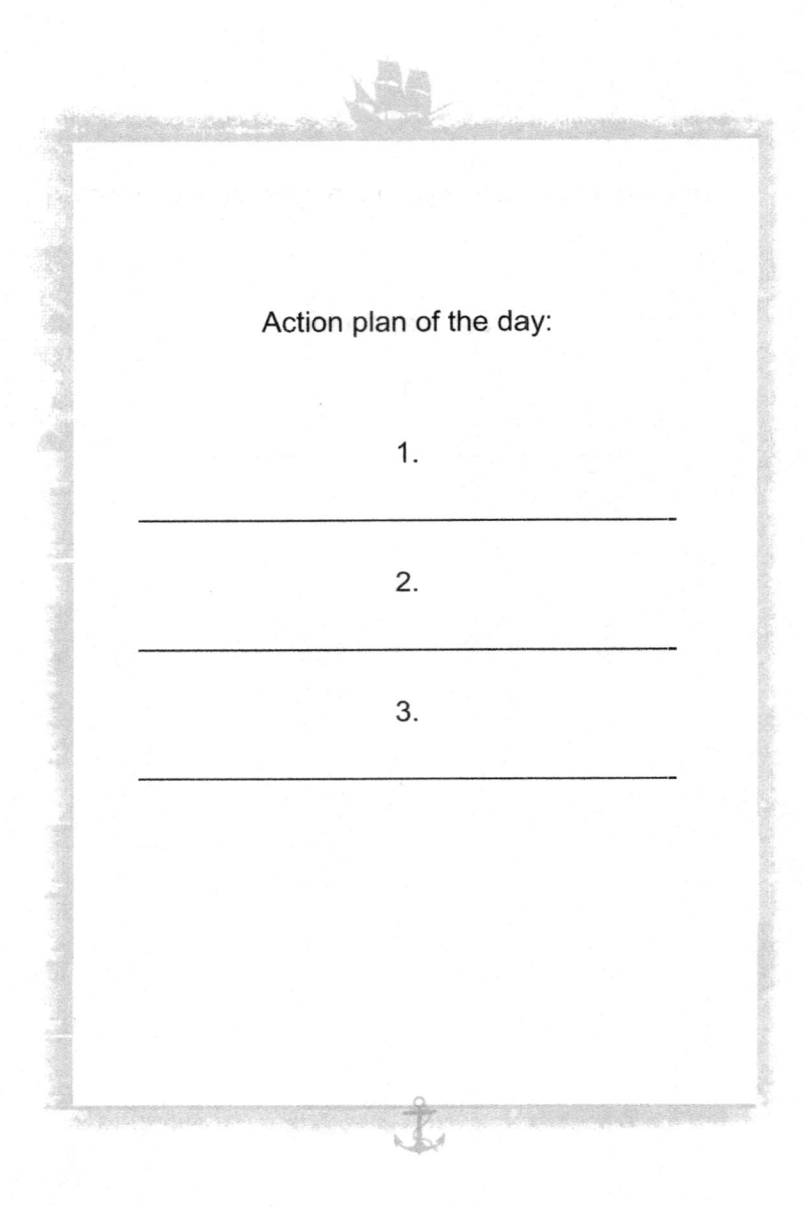

1.
_____

2.
_____

3.
_____

The Master Plan

To achieve this I will need to do:

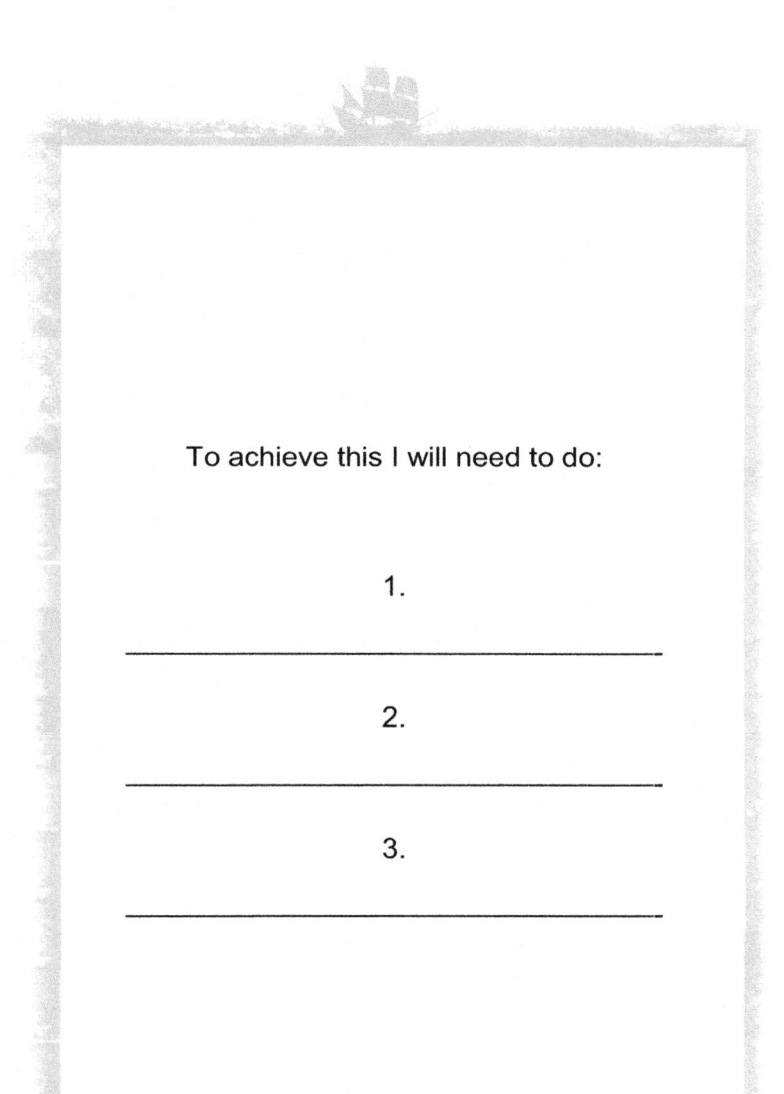

1.
_____

2.
_____

3.
_____

The Master Plan

Best thing that happened today:

_____

Struggles of the day:

1.

_____

2.

_____

3.

_____

The Master Plan

Solution for the struggles

1.
_____

2.
_____

3.
_____

Rate your day: (circle)

1 2 3 4 5 6 7 8 9 10

Are you closer to your goal: (circle)

Yes No

The Master Plan

Final thought of the day:

_____

Seven-day review: (one page every 7 days)

Did I hit my 7-day goal: (circle)

Yes   No

The Master Plan

Things that worked over the past 7 days:

1.
_____

2.
_____

3.
_____

How to keep winning:

1.
_____

2.
_____

3.
_____

The Master Plan

What I struggled with the past 7 days:

1.

_____

2.

_____

3.

_____

How to fix these struggles:

1.

_____

2.

_____

3.

_____

The Master Plan

Over all week:

1 2 3 4 5 6 7 8 9 10

Next 7 day goal:

The Master Plan

Congratulations!

You have made it to your first 28-day goal!

How does it feel?

What was your takeaway?

The Master Plan

Please write me, I'd love
to hear your personal success story.

Email me at:

johnedwardgillespie@gmail.com

Or list my website:

Johnnygillespiemusic.com

Ig
@johnnygmusic

The Master Plan

The Master Plan

Made in the USA
Coppell, TX
01 February 2024